D1567491

Published by the Freedom From Religion Foundation
PO Box 750 | Madison, WI 53701
FFRF.org | 608-256-8900

Copyright © 2019 Freedom From Religion Foundation
All Rights Reserved

ISBN: 9781877733178
Library of Congress Control Number: 2019937756

Select images of Don Addis cartoons are copyright Times Publishing
Company and are reprinted with express written permission. These select
images include cartoons found on pages 25, 32, 33, 35, 36, 37, 38, 39,
41,42, 45, 46, 48, 49, 79, 95, 96, 106, 114, 115, 146, 147, 149.

FFRF thanks the Times for granting permission to reprint Andrew
Meacham's column, "Cartoonist's Wit Was Mightier than the Sword,"
originally appearing in The St. Petersburg Times on Dec. 1, 2009.

FFRF is also grateful for cartoons provided courtesy of the Center
For Inquiry.

The vast majority of cartoons in this book were drawn by Don Addis for
FFRF's use and are licensed to FFRF.

EDITOR Annie Laurie Gaylor

GRAPHIC DESIGNER Jake Swenson

PHOTOGRAPHER Brent Nicastro

Cartoons for the Irreverent

Celebrating the Wit of Don Addis

Published by the Freedom From Religion Foundation

Contents

Introduction

Don Addis — An Irreverent 'Fly on the Wall'

By Annie Laurie Gaylor

Sometime in the early 2000s, editorial cartoonist Don Addis began surprising me with a few original drawings of cartoons that had recently appeared in the St. Petersburg Times. Don had been a longtime member of the Freedom From Religion Foundation, and I was then editor of FFRF's newspaper, Freethought Today. These cartoons contained Don's irreverent jibes at religion, religious politicians and the Religious Right — going after the incessant assault against reason, secular government and the Enlightenment. It was fascinating to examine the black and white originals to see Don's craft at work: the faint underlines of the original pencil sketch, the occasional whiteouts, and other markings showing Don's very pure technique.

As co-founder of the Freedom From Religion Foundation, I had long realized that editorial cartoonists were FFRF's best friends. In the 1970s, 1980s and well into the '90s, before the growth of the secular movement, it was almost unheard of to run into a reporter or columnist — or a famous person — who would admit to being a nonbeliever, much less be willing to associate with FFRF. Our saviors were editorial cartoonists like Don Addis, with their rapier wit, who told it like it is.

Sadly, after drawing cartoons six days a week for 40 years, Don was "retired" in 2004, like so many of our nation's roster of talented, satiric, watchdog editorial cartoonists.

Don Addis.

Don was born on Friday the 13th, 1935, and, being a good superstitionist, arranged to officially retire on Friday the 13th. An Army veteran, Don was a graduate of the University of Florida, where he edited a humor magazine. Don later wrote a monthly humor column for the Sunday Perspective section. One of his famous one-liners was: "Where do card-carrying nudists carry their cards?"

A 1988 feature in the St. Petersburg Times described Don this way:

"He paints faces on rocks. He collects stuffed gorillas. He keeps a false nose in his work drawer. One of his ancestors invented the toothbrush (maybe). He likes chess, crossword puzzles and palindromes. He juggles. He paints. He makes home movies (or used to). He mumbles, he paces and sometimes stares out the window. He listens to Mozart and Beethoven. . . . He doesn't care for politicians or Bucs [Buccaneers] football. Gun fetishists, creationists and bathroom humor are not high on his list, either."

Don Addis accepting FFRF's Freethought In the Media "Tell It Like It Is" award from Annie Laurie Gaylor, then editor of Freethought Today, at FFRF's 2005 national convention in Orlando. The plaque engraving included a reproduction of Don's signature fly.

In his farewell column in 2004, Don Addis addressed those who complained over the years that his work was not balanced or objective: "Objectivity is not my department. Balance is down the hall. Impartiality is another word for no reason to draw a cartoon."

The Freedom From Religion Foundation gave Don our Freethought in the Media "Tell It Like It Is" award at FFRF's 2005 national convention in Orlando, Fla., where I got to meet him in person. He was a quiet, shy guy. His former wife accompanied him to his award presentation. Don agreed to accept the award in person, but told me in an email: "My drawings do my talking . . . no speechifying. That's not negotiable." We agreed that following an introduction about him, after which he would accept a plaque on stage, we would simply show his cartoons, which did indeed speak for him. What could be better?

Don's email moniker was *inkyfeller@aol.com*, and we corresponded briefly over the years through email about business matters, but once I asked him about the ubiquitous fly appearing in most of his toons. He explained it was an inside joke with his mother-in-law, which continued even after she became his former mother-in-law, which shows you what kind of guy he was. Dan Barker, my husband and FFRF co-president, likes to speculate that Don was that "fly on the wall." (We had the engraver reproduce one of Don's signature flies on his award plaque, a touch Don enjoyed.) I also asked Don how many of his cartoons had been published. He put it at well over 11,150. This collection represents a bit more than a mere 1 percent of his life's work.

When he retired in August 2004, the editorial page editor of the St. Petersburg Times, Philip Gailey, wrote a lovely tribute to Don. Gailey explained that they were devoting an entire op-ed page to Don's cartoons but that, unfortunately they didn't have the full collection to draw upon. "Don," his editor noted, "being the soft touch he is, would give an original cartoon to everyone who asked for it." I can attest that he would send you the original even if you didn't ask for it — he apparently distributed his originals like gifts to those he saw as sympatico.

Gailey concluded: "Our board meetings will be a little more serious but not nearly as much fun without Don, who gave us what opinion pages are short on — a light touch. We will miss him a lot, and he leaves with our great affection and respect and gratitude. I don't know exactly what Don has in mind for his retirement years, but I have a feeling he is not about to stop making people smile."

His editor had that right. In retirement, Don went into overdrive. He began penning cartoon after brilliant cartoon for Freethought Today and FFRF. Receiving Don's packets in the mail, filled with new, original cartoons drawn just for FFRF to publish, was the highlight of that day. I would gleefully go around the office to show off the latest offerings before we published them. My mother, Anne Nicol Gaylor, FFRF's principal founder, was a special admirer. (Her favorite is reproduced on this page, as well as on Page 49. The original is framed and hanging in the Diane Uhl Legal Wing in Freethought Hall, FFRF's office building in downtown Madison, Wisconsin.) Don created these cartoons for the love of it, to support our cause, and, I suppose, because he just couldn't stop telling it like it is on vital issues of the day after a lifetime of creating cartoons six or seven days a week. He still had so much to say, so many icons to clast. His retirement possibly held one silver lining for him. It gave him the license to focus on his favorite target: religion. Boy, did Don ever have a field day when "Intelligent Design" became the

subject of a court battle, *Kitzmiller v. Dover*. A whole hilarious chapter in this collection is devoted to the cartoons he drew for us about evolution, lampooning creationism and eulogizing Charles Darwin.

Don's cartoons are spare, witty, sometimes silly, usually elegantly simple — and deceptively gentle. Eventually, with Don's kind permission, we produced a wall calendar in 2008 featuring one cartoon per month, and oh, was it hard to narrow them down to only 12. We also selected a few favorites and framed them, where they are proudly on display in Freethought Hall.

In retrospect, the timing of that calendar was fortunate. Soon after it came out, Don reported that he had become sick. He told me there would be no more cartoons, but expressed the wish that Freethought Today would continue to re-use what we

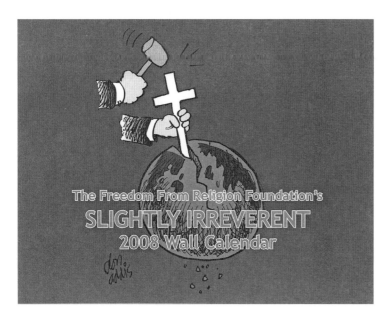

The Freedom From Religion Foundation's
SLIGHTLY IRREVERENT
2008 Wall Calendar

had in stock. He died at age 74 of lung cancer, at home, on Nov. 29, 2009.

Andrew Meacham, one of the St. Petersburg Times' staff writers, wrote a memorial column upon Don's death: "Cartoonist's Wit Was Mightier than the Sword," which is being reprinted in this book with permission. That article, which follows this introduction, documents Don's impressive editorial career, as well as providing some chuckles about Don, whom Meacham called a "lovable grump."

We have, as Don suggested, continued to print his cartoons over the years, but these gems largely have been tucked away unseen in an office file drawer. Every time I've gone through them, to search for a cartoon for this or that enterprise (including some full-page ads for FFRF we've run in several major newspapers), I would go from admiration and laughter to frustration over the fact that such wonderful cartoons were buried in a file drawer, when they are what the world needs to see. I'm ashamed it took me 10 years to realize that we could rescue these forgotten works of art and commentary by publishing them in this book, a long-overdue celebration of the irreverent cartoons of Don Addis.

Don's views on religion, science (mis)education and the Christian Right unfortunately remain as prescient and timely today as when he penned them. I'm especially fond of the toons found in the first chapter, "Is this thing on?" featuring his cartoons defending atheists and nonbelievers, and ridiculing how we are demonized. The chapters are loosely organized by content, and deal with science versus religion, feminism and gay rights, the dangers of the entanglement of state and church (which Don outdid himself with), and toons lampooning religion and true believers. The final chapter contains some of the more political of his cartoons in our collection, many going after George W. Bush, and they deserve resurrection, too, particularly his commentary about the shredding of the U.S. Constitution. One can only mourn the fact that we are denied knowing what Don would have had to say about another Donald now in the news.

In 2011, the St. Petersburg Times, one of the great U.S. dailies, changed its name, becoming the Tampa Bay Times. Our special thanks to the Tampa Bay Times board, which includes members who knew and admired Don personally, and understood what we seek to accomplish in honoring Don with this book. The board gave permission to reprint a couple dozen cartoons that originally appeared in the St. Petersburg Times, and to reprint

Meacham's column about Don. Warm thanks as well to Free Inquiry, published by Center for Inquiry, which also allowed us to reprint cartoons Don had penned expressly for them, including many of the delightful cartoons found in Chapter 7 on women's and gay rights.

Aside from possessing the talent to caricature and render an "aha" moment with artistic economy of style, you have to be really clever — maybe a genius — to be a great editorial cartoonist. Editorial cartoons say so much with so few words, or no words at all, "connecting the dots" to create that (secular) epiphany. Editorial cartoonists have no loyalties — except to the truth, and that makes them vital voices in our nation. But these voices have alarmingly dwindled. According to the Herb Block Foundation, at the start of the 20th century, there were about 2,000 editorial cartoonists working for newspapers. By the 1980s, according to NPR, there were about 300 staff cartoonists. By the end of 2008, there were fewer than 100. The carnage continues. The shocking statistic as of early 2019 is that there may only be 50 or fewer staff cartoonists left at U.S. daily newspapers.

Ted Rall, a former head of the Association of American Editorial Cartoonists, has pointed out that you know a newspaper is in trouble if the staff cartoonist gets the ax. Steve Benson, when he was laid off after nearly 40 years as the Arizona Republic's editorial cartoonist in 2019, quipped to the Washington Post: "Cartoonists are canaries in the coal mine — and we draw darned good canaries." Daryl Cagle, a cartoonist who runs Cagle Syndicate, calls editorial cartoonists "an endangered species."

The independent views of these hugely talented critics and commentators — whose offerings used to be the first item many of us turned to in reading a newspaper — are being extinguished. And our nation and democracy is by far the worse for this mass extinction.

If you can make someone laugh about a controversial subject, aren't you halfway there to converting them to your point of view? This collection of cartoons by Don Addis brings a smile, while making us think. I hope you will enjoy as much as I do this chance to savor the irreverent sampling of Don Addis' cartoonery, wit and wisdom.

Annie Laurie Gaylor is a co-founder of the Freedom From Religion Foundation, serving, with Dan Barker, as co-president.

Photography by Brent Nicastro

In Memoriam
Cartoonist's Wit Was Mightier than the Sword

By Andrew Meacham

Originally published on Dec. 1, 2009, in the
St. Petersburg Times. Reprinted with permission.

More than once, some cartoon Don Addis had drawn would outrage a politician's constituents, who would vent their displeasure on Mr. Addis or his employers, the Evening Independent and then the St. Petersburg Times.

Then the politician would drop him a note: "Loved the cartoon — can I have the original?"

Mr. Addis kept grinding out black ink drawings for 40 years for both papers, admiring the politicians' thick skin while cultivating one of his own.

Even the occasional death threat didn't bother him, his family said.

A burly man who collected stuffed gorillas and leather football helmets, Mr. Addis treated readers in hundreds of newspapers as well as Playboy magazine to his quirky window on the world, which colleagues describe as that of a "lovable grump."

Mr. Addis, the creator of several nationally syndicated comic strips, including the award-winning "Bent Offerings," died Sunday of lung cancer. He was 74.

"He operated at a megahertz not many people do," said daughter Alice Addis, 46. "We thought he was so intelligent that he suffered having to be around us mere mortals."

Even so, the man who loved chess and stocked his bookshelves with skeptical philosophy and the works of Einstein was not above a silly play on words. In one representative frame, a pipe-smoking general with sunglasses holds an empty leash: "Dogless MacArthur."

Mr. Addis started in 1964 as a cartoonist for the Independent, the afternoon paper and direct rival to the Times. The Florida Education Association gave him four straight School Bell Awards, starting in 1969, for "sharp wit and stinging satire."

In 1974, the Times and Independent were named Best Illustrated Newspapers in a statewide contest, with Mr. Addis taking first place in cartooning to third place for the Times' Jack Barrett.

"It was a friendly rivalry," said retired Independent reporter Rick Rutan. "The Times was big-city stuff, and we were the people's newspaper."

Mr. Addis became an important part of the camaraderie at the Independent, where he had established himself as the office curmudgeon. His chess games with reporter Jon Wilson could take weeks to complete.

To bolster morale, he set up a "graffiti board" in the editorial office, encouraging staffers and their bosses to drop by and vent even their smallest frustrations.

"It was things that wouldn't make the newspaper," said Rutan, 83. "Out-of-pocket stuff."

Mr. Addis also worked out of an upstairs studio in his 1920s vintage house in west St. Petersburg. He was a prolific freelancer who sold his first cartoon to Playboy in 1959, his last in 1999. In 1962 he created the magazine's "Symbolic Sex" feature.

He launched several strips for syndication, starting with "Briny Deep" in 1980. Briny, "a nautical Snuffy Smith in a sea cap," he said, sailed for two years with zany cohorts Salty Scrimshaw and Moby Dip, but ran aground when readers failed to identify.

"The Great John L," a strip about a playground fighter that replaced Briny in 1982, was distributed to 700 newspapers and lasted for another few years.

He launched his most successful venture, the single-frame "Bent Offerings," in 1988. In 1993, the National Cartoonists Society bestowed its annual award for newspaper panel cartoons to Mr. Addis for the feature.

Readers did not always appreciate his humor. One reader from Wesley Chapel, offended by a cartoon about elderly golfers, called his work "obtuse, silly, or in some cases gratuitously insulting."

Sometimes, the feeling was mutual. Over the decades, Mr. Addis listened to countless readers calling in with ideas for cartoons. "He hated it when they came up with cartoon ideas," Rutan said.

At the same time, Mr. Addis knew he was fortunate to have a job he enjoyed, his family said.

Mr. Addis grew up in Hollywood, Calif., and Hollywood, Fla. As editorial cartoonist for the Alligator at the University of Florida, "he got the message across so effectively it made my editorials superfluous," said Jim Moorhead, the Alligator's editor, who would later join Mr. Addis for years at the Independent.

Though loyal to friends and family, Mr. Addis was not gregarious. While others partied though the holidays, he preferred to stay home with a book, where a welcome mat still reads "GO AWAY." He bought smelts for an egret in the neighborhood, which stalked him regularly.

Mr. Addis died at home, preferring family members to hospice care. A colleague, former Independent editor of editorials Michael Richardson, eulogized Mr. Addis in an email for his "bearable arrogance born of his genius, his incomparable insight into the foibles of humanity, his occasional flirtations with humility, and in his great years the piercing knack of provoking wit due not merely to mocking the intolerable but piercing the truth."

Biography

Donald G. Addis

Born: Sept. 13, 1935

Died: Nov. 29, 2009

Survivors: daughters Eileen Wilson, Alice Addis and Mary Addis; son Douglas Addis and his wife, Christi; brother Tom Addis; four grandchildren.

Chapter 1
Voice of Reason

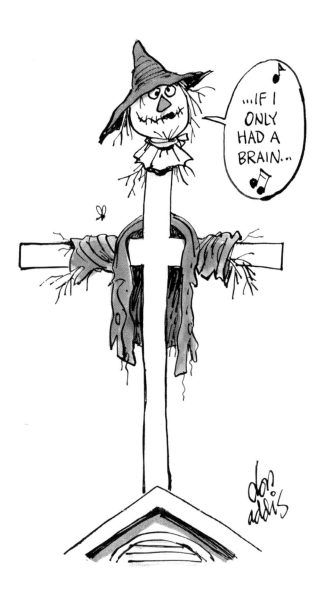

Chapter 2
Church/State: Fatal Attraction

ONE NATION, UNDER GOD

GOING NOWHERE

Chapter 3
How to Spot a True Believer

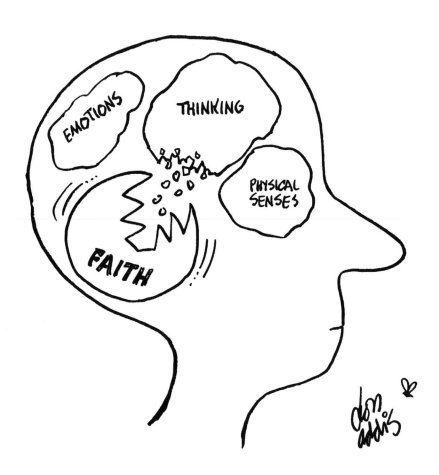

Chapter 4
Evolving

"ID" tag

MASTER OF DISGUISE

THE LATEST KNOCK-KNOCK JOKE

Chapter 4: **Evolving** | 81

Chapter 5
Science vs Religion

WHAT HATH GOD ROT?

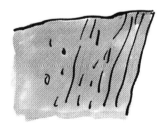
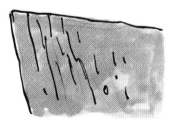

Chapter 6
Get a Load of the Religious Nuts

GREAT OAKS
FROM LITTLE
ACORNS GROW

CENTURIES-OLD
IGNORANCE AND
SUPERSTITION

GROUNDED IN TRADITION

Chapter 7
Welcome, Ladies, to the 21st Century

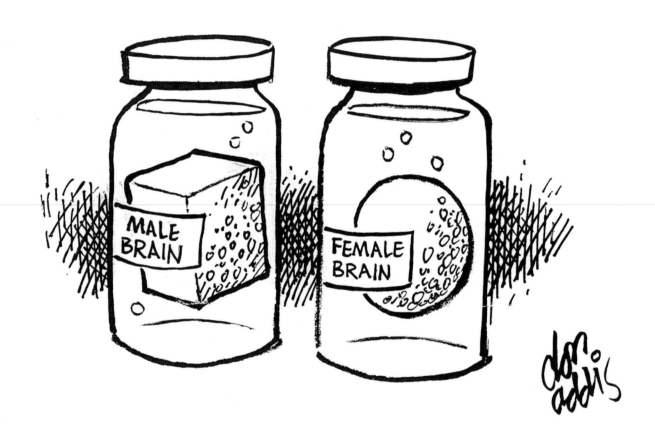

Chapter 8
Majority Rule

LAME DUCK MOMENTS

THE NEW FOUR HORSEMEN ... PLUS ONE

POSTMODERN MAN

The End